Whose hand would you like to hold...

Patricia McCarthy

AGENDA EDITIONS

ISBN 978-1-908527-38-7

First published in 2020 by

Agenda Editions
Harts Cottage,
Stonehurst Lane,
Five Ashes,
Mayfield,
East Sussex
TN20 6LL

Front cover image:
Fragment from a medieval Doom window,
St. Mary's Church, Ticehurst

Design and production by JAC design
Crowborough, East Sussex TN6 1DH

Printed and bound in Great Britain by
T J Books Ltd, Padstow, Cornwall

Patricia McCarthy, editor of *Agenda* (agendapoetry.co.uk) won the National Poetry Competition 2013. She is half Irish and half English. Her formative years were spent in County Dublin and County Wicklow. After graduating from Trinity College, Dublin, she lived in Washington D.C., Paris, Kathmandu, Dhaka and Mexico. She was Head of English for several years at Mayfield School, and has lived for many years now in the countryside in East Sussex.

Her poems have been/are being widely published in newspapers, journals and anthologies both in the UK and Ireland.

Certain poems here have appeared, or are about to appear, in *Acumen, Poetry Salzburg Review, The Wild Court, Poetry* and *All That Jazz* (South Downs Poets) and *The High Window*.

'Every Summer' was *Acumen*'s chosen featured poem of the week. 'Ice-Child' was inspired by a painting of the same name by Elizabeth Hannaford and features in her solo exhibition, 'Green World Burning' (Broken World Series) in Westminster Reference Library, put on hold because of the Corona virus.

The High Window made the sequence a special feature, with a commentary and several poems on its website, thanks to David Cooke

With special thanks to William Bedford for his very careful, inspirational, constructive advice, and to both him and Grey Gowrie for their encouragement in the making of this sequence.

Many thanks also to Marcus Frederick for his detailed editorial suggestions.

Thanks also to Josephine Evans for her photograph on the front cover.

Prologue

Draw the curtains, light the candle.
Time to sit as the Brontes did,
the wind rattling its commentary

to windows and doors – as if ghosts
of loved ones crave re-entry.

Time to make up once-upon-a-times,
ever-afters, happy or not, and, turn
by turn, to sharpen narrative skills

on the fire's licking flames. Knights
and knaves from *Gondal* are here still,

worlds wait to be peopled and placed
from *Angria*, *Glass Town* – Diary papers
and Charlotte's *Roe Head* journal

to blend fiction with fact. Take out
your pens and paper, fill old inkwells

and, for your own wobbly cursives,
become graphologists, deciphering more
about your selves than ever you knew.

Emily's fierce faithful dog, Keeper,
on guard in your psyches, will escort you

over your minds' wildest moors.
No need for heather, rocky crags – simply
fall over the edges of your temperament

into each story's special balm. The sisters –
and even the brother – will experiment

with you in travelling without moving
to emulate, in a villa, the writers
of *The Decameron* who reeled off tales

to avoid epidemics of fear in a plague
far off. There, your shared travails

might compose tragedies, no soaps,
around Branwell's call-girls and drink,
Charlotte's obsession with a married man...

Fight off the attacker. Emily will scribble –
with yours – her secrets, fast as she can.

The night clear, silent, the stars
clarifying themselves into faces
of those gone before in plagues
from the Occident – Mers, Sars.

No planes above, just geese
honking under a crescent moon,
Venus bright as a searchlight
over all lives henceforth on lease.

Morning might bring its mask
of fog, blurring even the outlines
of oaks, branches turned into tines

on fate's wheel that stops and starts
at random. No one knows whose head
will fall, which valley fill with the dead.

Dusks and dawns, keens of Canada geese
over the closed heads of cuckoo flowers
and celandines, their wings' satin swish

sweeping the sky, as if they don't want
the stars to print their astrological charts
on fields where crop circles still mystify

and black ley lines signify simple disasters.
This: more cataclysmic. As if the geese –
in v-shaped skeins, or two by two –

know something undefined, unwritten,
invisible is hanging over us. See them
wipe off the squashed-up faces of the stars.

iii

Geese, geese, your squawks now wails
haunt us as if you are the banshee
white as nenuphars in graveyards.

Tell us where and when we went wrong.
Did we not find a pond for you wide
as the five oceans to settle into so you

could stop parping that you don't belong.
There, amongst fronds, blue and yellow flags,
you can never be locked in, shut down,

all your water-windows imprinted with sky.
With Venus no longer our guide, grant us
man's oldest wish: the means you have to fly.

Holy week, our childhood voices singing
Gregorian chant far off, nuns' rosaries
chinking as thuribles fill with incense,

hands with candles. Under a blue moon
only, we genuflect – while sirens wail
in emptied city streets through silences

that echo for miles. Long have we swapped
naves for woodland paths, treading in
imprints of a man who shouldered everyone

on his way to the cross: a man we need
urgently to help us here where ash dieback
matches the dieback of people who run out,

even, of mountain air. Maybe it is his heart
beating in every tree, his pulse in throats
of nightingales still too soon to find

in the early April season. We daub foreheads
with ash from old bonfires. Spy Wednesday,
Maundy Thursday, Good Friday: cross

after cross, masks stolen by thieves
from wards where eyes of the paralysed
on ventilators stay open all night

unseeing, comatose. We do not hear.
the tapping of nails into flesh and wood.
Our girlhood voices suddenly lack a tune.
Nothing to sing about under this blue moon.

Pink Super-Moon, in between worm moon
and flower moon, who are you as you loom
over lands far and wide with all your names:

sprouting grass moon, egg moon, fish moon.
Do you let the traditional plaits of children
in reservations swing like metronomes over you,

your rhythms and tides given to wigwams
and clearings, your colour absorbed
from their wild ground-phlox as it spreads

widely into Spring after Spring. Do you
signify the end of the world as we know it,
your appearance dangerously close to the Earth

that laughs in your face, showing off blossoms,
shivers of green in silver birches, oaks –
no trace of the plague. Or can you see

behind what appears, decipher ancient scripts
of almanacs and bibles, a dreamt-up quatrain
by Nostradamus about a queen from the east

causing an uncontrollable endemic, men
turned into the dust that tints and covers you?
Pink Super-Moon, restore in life our trust.

This cottage has known it before:
its long cold room with its musty air
offered as a mortuary, sin-eaters
chanting outside and glorified bodies
inside souls escaping, soot-coated,
up wide chimney-breasts with ghouls
of non-believers. Rats, like now,
more numerous than people, circus acts
performed by fleas on their backs
before their leaps onto putrified skin
of the few still living. Wet nurses,
wheelwrights, blacksmiths, physicians
tired from rubbing onions, herbs
and chopped-up adders onto boils,
wiping hung pigeons over infected bodies,
giving draughts of ten-year old treacle
and vinegar, offering even urine
to sip as fevers rise, buboes
swell and multiply. No one
in the streets except a few flagellating
themselves to escape what they think
is the wrath of god. A stench everywhere
in that long lockdown. No running water,
tin pails for excretion, outside pumps dry.

Lessons to learn from shut doors
about the blackest Black Death's cure.

Ring a ring of roses: a pocket full of posies...
From the fourteenth century
he appears through cob walls,
clothed in night's black skins, dots of fleas

leaping from pest to person. The biggest rats
are on his hands, leather gloves
keeping him from contamination.
No use the sharp-toothed, circling feral cats,

nor the doctors, priests, exorcists, undertakers
between partitions of wattle and daub –
where corpses, globed by carbuncles,
are infectious, open fires no deliverers

from colonies for which his shadow roots.
He talks of traps, of loose bait:
green poisoned beads of wheat
in tunnels he plans for the vermin to loot.

He searches for planks in nettles, tiles stripped
by winds for these pig descendants
reluctant to be his, or anyone's victims.
He swills away pails in which they have dipped

and hires himself out, half-wanting reprieve
from his rat-catcher rôle. He knows
they jump not at his throat but at the light –
on the lookout for Pied Pipers who will believe

they can lead children over their own runs
and scrapes into underground caves
to be petted for their intelligence and fur.
Unnerved by his eyes, I don't tell of skeletons

haunting the stair, of scratchings in beam and bone.
A ghost of myself in these precincts,
I avoid all the centuries with him
I have forgone. *Atishoo, atishoo. We all fall down.*

A different epidemic: polio, nineteen fifties.
From Fawley Refinery with its torch-flare
to Lyndhurst where verderers brand wild ponies –
children, the victims of this spike, call for witches

to sweep the disease away with brooms,
imagining it a usual forest fire. Doors bang
to shut village schools, dropped pigtail-ribbons
flutter in playgrounds where skipping rhymes sang

to the sky. A small girl is lying by a window
on a narrow bed, a tartan rug thrown over her –
days and nights twilit as, pulse racing, then slow
she fights for her life. On guard, like an angel,

her mother lays ice-cold cloths over her forehead
to bring down the fever. On the wireless, *Listen*
with Mother distracts from news of those paralysed,
of numbered casualties, and tiny coffins that glisten

in the sun, ready, it seems, to put on merrygorounds,
not to sink into the soil; calipers, crutches, wheelchairs
in short supply. Everywhere is out of bounds –
tiny faces peering, as if from Advent calendars,

from communal iron lungs. My sisters make funny faces
against the glass pane. For I am that critically ill small girl.
My semi-formed scribble leaves wide, paper spaces
in the squares of every fragile day when I try to keep up

with *Bushy Squirrel's Diary*. Pictured in the margin:
the shy red squirrel seeing off the rat-like grey.
When I am too weak, my mother fills in
the doctor's visits, the doses of M&B, the moments

I collapse and they think they have lost me....
'Toreador' blasts from the gramophone's trumpet.
Outside, playmates hide behind a wall of sweet peas.
The cricket field's three-legged races, the arrows

chalked on winding lanes where we play Tracking,
old Will's pigs, the lily ponds… are still there.
So is the polio. It contaminates the rigging
of oil tankers and tar brought in by tides on Lepe Beach.

There we used to watch ocean-going liners pass
through The Solent: the two Queens, the green Caronia.
Luckier than most, I am left with horn-rimmed glasses,
a patch over a lazy eye and weekly appointments

in a hospital where I have slides: parrots to place
in cages, elephants in compounds… No graphs, like now,
of peaks, plateaus and R rates, yet the same race –
beyond horizons that tie themselves in knots – for a cure.

Let us hope magi, priestesses and witch doctors agree
on a vaccine simple as the one then found: dissolved
in a sugar cube. Meanwhile verderers round up the ponies,
birchwood brooms, in a gorse-glow, fight the forest fires.

Think, now, whose hand you would like to hold:
for the last time: that of a secret or lost lover,

maybe, whom you always believed you would see
again one day. But now 'one day' has arrived.

And ask yourself why, O why – with roads closed,
planes parked and passenger ships in dock –

you deliberately locked yourself down out of fear,
respect or shyness; why you were not wilder – as loss

upon loss piles up in a makeshift mass grave dug
by your spade over the years, finality the dreaded find.

Think, now, of the faces you cherish – those
that shadow-gatherers have half-stolen – and recall

the arias in your soul when you topped yourself up
with them, the illuminated initials of each word

of theirs, the cobalts, coppers, golden centres
in their eyes that enchanted yours, the touching often

without touch. Reflect on those stolen moments
of grace; re-live them despite your skin-hunger.

No longer can you be resigned to carving them into
the ghosts you dwell with. For what of the endearments

not uttered, the lifetimes missed, choices
not taken in countries you could have named

while composing cantos for rivers, new summits
for mountains. Remember, the heart

never ages, even in rags; silences speak in colour.
Yet, in a blink, a second belongs to the past

which dissolves into a dream, impermanence
all you can cling to. So why not collect horizons

on which to write lines of poetry for recitals
in the ether, away from this clumsy-graceful dance

on earth. And think whose hand you would like
to hold one last time, then press softly to your lips.

Many tales untold not for the telling
within four walls, no escape, under the skin.
Tatooed on minds, they wrinkle the heart
with fear, with rankle, hardly worth
lip-service... *tell tale a tattler* you sing...
buy a penny rattler... to deafen their din
in nights when owls pull dreams apart
and caterwauls relay the dearth
of birdsong, claws sharpened on moons.
O the tales within tales gagged at the start
bubble in vats with a flick and a stir
into *telltales for the tattler* – not forgotten:

Give it to the man; never take it back sir.

Tell tales. If only it was just that
and you could pass it off as nonsense,
jibber-jabber, as the oldest wives' tales.
Far worse when his tirade arrives.
You know every single line off pat
as if a prompter off stage, silence
your refuge lest you incense what he exhales,
and you try to imagine your many lives
surrounded by a circle of protection
as he downs pint after pint. *Tell tale
a tattler,* yes *telltaleatattler* Please let
his slurs be skipping rhymes in repetition,
not swearwords, curses, insults to wittle.
Tittle tattler, shake like hell the *rattler*.

I want you to hold me
always
as if a forest fire raged
around me,
tongues and tongues
coming at me
but only your flame
to ignite me
into colour
without scorch marks
or ashes.

I want you to hold me
always
as if I were your first woman
ever,
as if I were the most forbidden:
the secret
longest-kept behind your eyes;
as if I were your fantasy:
a composite woman
you could not take
your hands off.

I want you to hold me
always
as if there is no tomorrow,
no other day
or night
in which to touch.
I want you to hold me
as if
there has never been
or could be
any other.

Suddenly I am becoming you:
my mother: your smile in the corners
of my mouth, my lips never quite able
to achieve that Cupid's bow of yours.

Your falls like mine – in flutters
like leaves from a rustling tree –
over dips in concrete, broken drains
as you raced up and downhill.

Where I sat with you on hard chairs
at hospital appointments, I wait
for myself, now, without a daughter
or any next of kin. Yet I guard

a similar fireside, hear you offer
cups of tea in my voice. The wind
through my window transmits,
still, your advice, timelessly mocking

the nine decades you managed.
In the photograph just found,
of your fresh, girlish form
in the Trossachs, I discover a you

I never knew, very like the girl
I was, lost, almost, from memory.
And I watch them join hands,
scrying into futures not aghast

at this virus until, suddenly, I am you,
our bones knit together, wrapped
in all our ages in waiting rooms,
purple heather to rest our feet upon.

What, now, if my mother was there,
like many mothers, dignified, noble
advising me on my life even though

in her ninth decade, imprisoned
by long legs that cannot walk
any longer, her mind sharp as when

she did my homework aeons ago
and came out always on top,
myself a guilty imposter, What now

if her smile lingers there: that
of a beauty forty years younger –
who hoodwinked the eye specialist

into thinking her not down on his list
as he had in mind someone feeble,
decrepit, hunched over, What, now,

if she were to cower under bedclothes
from what resembles a bauble
on a Christmas tree or sputnik, and clap,

Thursday evenings, front-line staff
who do not know she was a key worker
once, in the days before antibiotics,

how she went by boat to nurse victims
of cholera, smallpox, leprosy, with no mask,
goggles or special gown, simply

a starched white uniform. During
the last three of her years, in the Home,
how carefully I dabbed rouge

on her high cheekbones, bought
her favourite Chanel lipstick, moisturiser
from Elizabeth Arden – while a carer

from the Philippines lovingly manicured
her nails and an architect and a philosopher
from Poland – employed for a pittance –

swapped, with her, their stories. How I hated
her residence there, but played when I could
the grand piano in the lounge where,

for patients that slumped, I transformed
its metallic honky-tonk tone
into her favourite pieces by Mozart,

Schubert, Debussy, my unpractised hands
losing their shyness in order to entertain.
What, now, if my mother was there,

ultra-precious for having lived so long,
like many mothers, visited only by
an unauthorised silent invader. What now?

The forgotten ones who have forgotten themselves:
see them stare out behind barred windows,
locked down in their bodies year after year.

What do they know of this virus that, cashing in
on their vulnerability, would sweep like a tsunami
through their insides with a roar, leaving them

with no higher ground to run to, no language
even to cry out, the tide pulling back every word
they once had, ransacking the familiar.

They are accustomed to intruders hiding behind
curtains, leaping out from flower pots, to ancestors
lurking upstairs when there is no upstairs

Yet since they are so certain of what they see
that their terror magnifies if they are queried,
their carers embroider their surreal images:

Yes, yes, there is a goblin in the wardrobe
and now he is creeping under your bed,
about to climb into your jug, your dressing-gown.

The forgotten ones who have forgotten themselves,
hollowed out by brain-disease, would they
wish to be saved, outside the land of the sane?

Only the little ghost of her it was,
wandering about her own bones whose density
had gone, her thoughts like Catherine wheels
whirring in her mind's shell. How we wished
to whisk her back before her illness
when, wed to her Clark Gable, her beauty
shone on the screen as, in wartime, for pin money,
she worked in the cinema, twirling reels
of Tom & Jerry, thrillers, the Pathé News.
Only the little ghost of her it was, our auntie,
dialling random numbers like lifelines.

A sense of danger lurked in the house
when you were there. Well-trod lands
beneath my feet shuffled back to maps,

unvisited, the furniture shrank against
walls for my bones to arrange themselves
in spaces suddenly architect-designed.

As shadows folded up into drawers,
and my profile tautened at your appraisal,
nothing was resigned. Masks I usually wore

hung from a peg cracked, so your gaze
could raid my face with impossible suggestions.
Sitting with you, I advanced somehow

into a clearing in the sky from which clouds
had retreated dancing. I suppose
I should have been wary of the place livening

at your laughter, of my fingers on the piano
managing the expression of some virtuoso –
while my skin thought you out and words,

shaking off their superfluities, fell
into your lap like dowries. Although, time
after time, I guessed each number in your head,

in a proven telepathy, I cherished not quite
recognising what your presence meant.
And, taking a bite from the blue moon,

I only know now without knowing how –
as then – despite distancing of lands and seas,
all my windows blaze impossibly with light.

We never knew what the ugly sisters did
to Cinderella – apart from shoving her
into the fire's ashes, bossing her to stoop
with a broom and scrubbing-brush to all
the menial chores. How carefully they hid
their abuse, treating her as an easy push-over
while they forced her into rags, made her scoop
up crumbs, and then forbade her the ball.

She never reported them, only too aware
they would have the last word and swear
it was simply acceptable aggression
by siblings, just rough-and-tumble play.
How many Cinderellas are there every day
afraid of retaliation, without a say?

We never know what goes on in tenements,
flats, houses between graffiti-covered walls
where half-sisters and step-sisters rival
each other with poisonous, vicious intent.
They steal make-up, jeans, adornments –
wearing jealousy's green horns – and call
each other names, headbutt, pinch – primeval
in strength, every foul rugby-tackle meant.

How many Cinderellas live in fear
of these Gonerils, Regans, Medusas with hair
that hisses snakes – and never dare
speak up, dreading tit-for-tat repercussions,
killer-punches of prize-fighters who call:
Mirror on the wall, we are the fairest of all.

You grazed nose to nose, belly to belly,
difficult to tell you apart, even though

you were one hand higher. From the start
you walked off together, no squeals,

kicks or pecking-order to establish
on her patch. You watched her die

outside her stable opposite yours,
and accepted it, much calmer than me,

wisdom in your instinct. You did not need
the chastetree berry, milk thistle, hops

I offered – to help you cope with her gone.
You lay where her sweet body was dragged

into the field. And you roll there still
for companionship when you have only

the summer sheep and the wind mounting you
in your season. A makeshift centaur, I give you

double the attention now: circle my fingers
on your rump to imitate her grooming

your velvet coat with her lips, my hair
her mane that you nuzzle. You snort

and sniff the air, as if you glimpse her
over the hedges, on the facing ridge

or expect her back down the garden path –
her bright bay, the white dot on her forehead

matching yours. Sometimes I think you
are her shadow, what she cast all those years

to follow her, elongated in evenings
of low suns. Yet, as she fills space,

you move again together, your kind eyes
sad mirrors in the meadow beyond.

Beware Beltaine: the maypoles
    flung into ditches, conspiracies
with white witches to kindle
    a near fire and a force fire
between which they drive the horses.
    Hear them creep out at midnight
over prints of fallow deer, the slime
    of toads – to cut swatches off the tails
of mares according to Wiccan rites.
    Look out for plaits in uncombed manes,
for twig crosses wound with hair –
    when tin-cans tilt through fleabane
towards opening and closing vulvas
    of mares in their first full season.
Catch them on the cusp of dawn
    as they stem the blood drawn to smear
their women with fertility, headcollars
    back on hooks, messages on rag trees –
while traumatised snorts haunt the breeze.
    Find, in the morning, dancing pumps
abandoned on the ground, sweat
    foaming on swollen hindquarters,
whites of eyes wild – silent covens,
    in retreat behind hedges, single file.
Beware Beltaine with its bluest bluebells.
    Suspect bonfires on hills and mounds,
deadly nightshade uprooted on banks,
    frenzied, ravaged whinnies at cults
of warlocks smoke-signalling their crimes.

Terrible to get the sun only by balancing
an arm or leg on a window-ledge,
worse if you have no head for heights –

and feel imprisoned with laws
forbidding you to go out. You dream
of prairies, seas, waving fields of wheat

but wake up to four solid walls,
flashing screens of ipads and computers
whose virtual worlds are no recompense.

You need pubs and bars and parks
more than the lucky few with lawns,
crazy-paving paths, wide-open back doors.

Eight o'clock, Thursdays. Instead
of racing to the fish-and-chip van
you clap your hands, cheer, bang pans

with all the residents along the street,
even chorus well-known songs, windows
lit-up stages for five-minute protagonists.

Somewhere, opera singers perform arias
heart-rending as the bows of cellists
and fiddlers who play from rooftops.

In a few soaring seconds, the have-nots
become the haves, crescendos, grace notes,
chords unifying every breath.

Ash before oak, we're in for a soak.
Oak before ash, we're in for a splash.

Splash it will be, then, the season
already demonstrating its visions
in the sun on fresh lime-green oaks,
in bluebells blurring the banks,
filling dells with cerulean seas,
badges of primroses almost gone.

Everything tender, innocent, new.
The Downs, rolling nearer into view,
invite you to walk as the crow flies
over lamb-dancing fields, no house
in sight, to a parallel world of 'then'
in which dog violets, stitchwort take you

away from the new disjointed normal
of 'now' – and return you to miracles
taken for granted before: the swallows
migrating over oceans and continents
back to the same rafters every year,
splashing walls a lucky white in stables;

wild ransoms scenting the copse – details
of natural cyclical rhythms that never fail
to reassure. Presences of those sacrificed –
wrapped around tree trunks and shadowing
still water – suggest that you, too, are
in a hereafter, eyes stripped of their scales.

Ash before oak, we're in for a soak.
Oak before ash, we're in for a splash.

My sister in France, newly widowed
and locked-down, in a double blow, I wonder
if the hedge-less scapes of seeded melons

and sunflowers in your view are enough for you;
if it is time to stop putting fresh flowers
daily on your husband's grave – and to close

the shutters as he used to do every sundown.
How I would like to bring you back to the bluebells
of our childhood, now, in badgers' wood;

to pick, with you, their liquid stems that used to fill
the baskets on our fairy bikes, our chanted spells
accompanied by the rattles of their chains

all the way home. You would find a surprise
of cowslips under a hedge as in the old meadows,
swish with your dress the flies in chainmail armour

off the grazing horse's face, then strut like a bride
along the single-track lanes whose verges are a show
of lady-smocks and cow-parsley lace.

You could hear again the first cuckoo, shyer
and rarer now than the ones we used to hear
and treasure all year round in cuckoo-clocks.

You could help the gypsy children on the corner
colour in their rainbows of hope with pastel crayons,
hang up garlands of wood-sorrel, barren-strawberry

on their gate, then try to catch their runaway cob
that has charged up the hill, a right goer of a trotter
ready for a race in Ireland. And you could walk, walk

walk – back through decades, from the here-and-now,
into space ages – everything happening forever,
and at once, chronological time bypassed.

My sister in France, you cannot fly here to be,
for the first time, a woman without a man – yet the heart
has its guardians, melody-tongued, whatever the country.

All I want: to drive round and around the M25
in a makeshift infinity, no turnings off,
your profile beside me as I hold your hand.

In the special, enclosed world of your leather-lined car,
we can shut out noise to glide over changing cambers,
the power-steering sensitive to your lightest touch

on destiny's wheel. All I want: to continue
round and around in our own world, safe between
hard shoulders in a suspended time, the rain outside

spattering the windscreen with its camouflage,
the wipers beating an easy duple rhythm for our hearts
to copy, describing intense careful arcs

for peering through. All I want: our voices
to emanate from the one mouth while we accelerate
round and around, regardless of mileages and signs

in your marathon-fit vehicle, your profile beside me,
your hand to hold within revolution upon revolution
of some spinning top. Know me by now, my darling.

I howl through hoops of a broken-down time
softly, openly, desperately, silently, beyond barriers
of both sound and safety at you indicating

right, left, slowing into a slipway – which implies
there will be no emergency services to help
when I lose, as lose I will, your hand, your profile;

when your presence cruises away down the fast lane…
And I am left to hitchhike alone back to where –
over double white lines, speed traps and cats' eyes –

you orbit, on the hospital bed of your death, around me.

See, they return, one and by one,
half-awakened to altered distances.

With tentative movements and slow feet
they cross Westminster Bridge, not quite yet

undone by death, the familiar brown fog
dissolved in the river's flow – along with

invisible masks of the faces behind faces
they unconsciously wore. Gone: the props

to the life they knew: lunch hours in cafés
careless with whom they mixed,

tankards raised outside a pub after work –
before the train home, standing room only.

Now their tracks seem to lead over peaks
and ash-coated plateaus – in their nightmares

men on Mars floating through airless wards.
See, they return, hesitant, uncertain,

preferring the cocoon of furloughed days,
fitted masks muffling efforts to talk.

The clarity in the dawn light fails to enlighten,
flickering off and on in their eyes shadowed

by the Terrible. Some want to trail
their limbs in the Thames as in the Ganges

for a new incarnation. Others aim to sprint
around the circumference of this estranged earth,

not realising they can make their mark simply
by being themselves, or overcoming themselves.

While forsaken corpses, each beloved to someone,
are piled high on shelves, too many for burial – .

see, they return, one by one, desperate
for transfigured destinies in the kingdom come.

Samson, Pagan, Mallory, Caesar,
Albert, Odin, Hero, Thor, Luna…

Luna I will call you, a moon mare
dyed chestnut by the setting sun.
Bolting, you must have tried to save
your injured rider from the brute force

of the protesters who, without a care,
hurled at you their ammunition.
Glass bottles, flares, bicycles gave
a reason for spooking to every horse,

especially you who needed moonlight
to sidestep them, with your crescents
of shoes, not the dim streets of disgrace.

No news of you, as if they want to efface
you from history. Scarred, tense,
misunderstood, you have, still, insight

into the moon's cycles of creation
and destruction while she waxes and wanes;
you hold her orbs in the whites of your eyes.
No one will replace your noble face

as, you stand, head down, without veneration,
at the back of your stable. Around the reins
tangled up in your legs I would tie
fresh-cut roses of Epona, protectress

of mounts like you, loyal slaves to humans –
and watch the petals drop when you lead
souls of every colour on their afterlife ride.

With your brave thoroughbred blood
steadied by Irish draught, you will abide
in hearts that run home and take no sides.

And turn your back on whoever is prejudiced
against you, who call you fizzy, a mad redhead.

Sefton, the famous, would grab the harsh curb
from your bit, whicker appreciatively instead.

Black, brown, dun, dappled grey, bright bay –
your mane moon-bleached into seeded hay.

The white climbing wedding roses
which have kept us waiting all year
are in full bloom around every pergola,
June their month. Yet no bride
wanders under their perfumed roof,

no groom, arms outstretched, poses
at the end of a passage, in fear
of thorns on thick stems. A pianola
seems to play itself from inside
a house, satin shoes tap proof

that ghosts of all the brides
who unstitched their gowns are asking
their beaux to lead them in a dance

over striped lawns – and to glide
through the unlived years' easings.
See how they dare the risk, this chance

to mingle in couples while petals fling
their confetti at each melting glance.

Every summer I half expect you.
I do not dare focus on too much detail –
your face, your shape silhouetted
with leaves against a noonday sun;
the years you've worn like armour
since last I saw you: inevitable changes.

Every summer I half imagine you
approaching from the skyline to hold me
in your words, looks and easy laughter
that resounds with steeples; concern
rucking horizons where trees, your trees, point
to the naked directions we planned to take.

Every summer I half espy you
in woods bunching wild garlic and celandines;
on ancient burial mounds where I was meant
to have done with you; at the top of tors –
kneeling to the wind, making the view
a vision wise with storytellers.

Every summer I half concoct you –
under stone arches where we still embrace,
in dreams that repeat like a maxim
the surety of loving you. Long grasses
on lane verges bow down to you. But
you never appear. And the summer, turning

inside out its dresses for you, is gone.

Always one that doesn't make it:
a single black wisp of down
on the concrete floor of the unused stable.

No safe landing in the wheelbarrow
filled with soiled wood-chips for the fledgling
fallen from a nest stuck to the purlin.

Yet today: such jubilation: baby swallows
singing and chattering a recitative to accompany
the opera diva on the radio playing all day.

Such forked-tail swoopings, soarings,
wild angles and wilder speed dared
with their new little wings, white bibs in the air,

the mare pricking her ears at the joy
of these new residents on her rafters, joists.
No spooks at the acrobatics over her head.

Simply, tuned into their performance,
she holds in reserve her musical-box whinnies
and whickers softly for me to join in.

In years to come, with fewer left on earth,
you will remind your children how daffodils,
one Spring, were trumpets played by angels,

how spiders' webs caught in the sun at dawn
had to unravel their filigree mandalas to string
violins for searingly sweet performances –

how arms of the bedridden lifted up and down –
across and back – in a ballet of catgut bows;
how conches picked up from a beach

became bugles through which sea-urchins blew
full orchestras out of street windows.
In years to come, with fewer left on earth,

you will scrub out the horrific – and ask
your children what they saw behind
see-through skies that suddenly were so clean,

and wonder if they heard you teach yourself
the cello, holding it between your legs
like the lover you didn't have until your skin

sank into its polished wood, and you hugged
and hugged it until you and the cello were one.
In years to come, in years to come...

What else can you be, child of our time –
except born and unborn in the ice
of a cap melting slowly,
greens and pinks of the northern lights
flowing through you instead of blood.

Cold, ice cold you are when, with too much
to feel, you find yourself up against
plagues, mass shootings, famines, knives:
with no trekking routes, no boats
over ice floes for rescue. I see you –

one eye closed against the intolerable,
the other squinting over sledge-prints
of Shackleton, Scott, North, South, picking –
off rock-like layers and levels of ice –
a husky's stiffened hairs to wrap about you.

Stay without flesh, child of our time,
guarded, in that foetal position, by as many
degrees below zero as you can stand.
The price of skin is vulnerability,
alienation. Freeze dreams of gardens

in your soul, and a mother's arms curved
into a sanctuary. Ignore the drip, drip
of water which kills off seals, polar bears –
and could kill you. May the silence
in your heart keep the song inside you.

Let us ask the wind to sigh for them,
then to strike up its orchestra in the trees:
a triumphal fanfare of elegies.

Let us ask the trees to cradle them
in their arms and give them their centuries
in retrospect – that they might choose histories

for their new lives of death wherein they might be
knights, troubadours, queens or kings:
in drove-ways, in rides, to the clap of wings.

Let us ask the fields to soften for them
into spring saffrons, emeralds, tropical limes –
and, at their interments, to offer them rhymes

of soil with root, of sward with sky.
The oaks' vaults will be their cathedrals,
aisles bind kicked leaves into hymnals.

Let us ask the seas to lay their syllables
upon them, until we travel over the waters
in the huge certainties their deaths have taught us.

Tread carefully. Decipher the geography
of the heart which will not be registered
on any map. See there its carving

by axe and by shovel, its snail-trails
that tempt with their silverings
yet lead nowhere. Tread softly

as if on butterflies' wings lest you disturb
their colours and patterns. Too much to lose
in the purified light between dawn and dusk

when seafarers scoop whole oceans
into their holds, Delphic caves are palaces
as well as prisons, and tribes relinquish rituals.

Tread carefully and softly in any easing.
Remember Egyptian, Tibetan, Celtic Books
of the Dead give spells to those interred

in an open grave – no epitaph on a stone,
no relative in sight, nor priest to anoint –
the silence doing its best to fill it in.

Then pause for a lover to do up your shoes,
not near enough to be near. While laces tie
and every creature alive bows down

in a brotherhood on the shifting earth,
the heart whispering its surest ways –
see even the wayward sink into tenderness.

Hear solos of barn-owls accompanying
woods which beat with the communal heart
of those lost, summer leaves the bunting

for a new 'normal' beyond non-stop knells.
Despite honeysuckle entwined around regrets –
the criss-cross of pollutant jet trails tells

of a sky-spoilt world gone back on itself.
The moon, in a haze, like a blank traffic-light,
neither red, green nor yellow tests the gulf

between then and now, lockdown and release.
Best to rely on the *anima mundi* which has
no language, but is Love feathered with Peace.

As lost beliefs stutter into creeds, its Grace
will not let those who died alone seem,
amidst Michaelmas daisies, to leave no trace.

All the farewells that could not be said,
are printing themselves over and over
on backs of swallows, word for shadow-word

flanked by ring-ouzels lest falcons snatch them
mid-flight. Mine amongst them, for my father,
spiral into a chorus of Creation psalms.

Epilogue

Draw back the curtains, snuff out the candle
and let Rilke's angels clean misted windows

with their wings, blowing glass into worlds
that, with a ring, break into our reflections.

Hear pavements crack when, wrapped in day,
they come and go from one gloryhole to another,

mythical rather than mystical, no longer overhead.
Personable, yet ordinary as tissues, they enjoy being

airbound with tight-lipped tidings, dodging fumes
that swirl into infinity, skiving from graves

and iron bedsteads. Natural recluses, they think out
our vacuities – and although small-boned as birds,

they offer large frameworks, digging from our voices
the unutterable to perfect into song. Hear them

dictate, from some castle turret, life-saving lines
on tracing paper. While lands change hands,

and shooting stars do u-turns, they call out
Fear and *Fear not*. The look on their faces is terrible.

Notes

Prologue:

'the attacker': the Brontes' attacker was tuberculosis; each in turn went into the 'decline' and died. The present attacker is Covid 19. Both are paralleled here and seen as one.

viii

By 1910, frequent epidemics became regular events throughout the developed world primarily in cities during the summer months. At its peak in the 1940s and 1950s, polio would paralyse or kill over half a million people worldwide every year.

Wikipedia

'the two Queens, the green Caronia': ocean liners – the Queen Elizabeth and the Queen Mary

x and xvii

The figures were uncovered by the London assembly as part of an investigation into abuse that found a 300% increase in half-sisters, grandmothers and stepsisters as offenders.

The figures from the Metropolitan police, who are investigating a rise in the number of domestic abuse offences committed by female family members, show that domestic abuse offences committed by sisters have doubled from 641 in 2010 to 1,325 in 2018. The numbers have quadrupled for stepsisters and half-sisters from 33 to 142.

The Guardian, April 14, 2020

xix

French police investigate wave of horse killings as satanic rituals suspected. At least 19 killings and mutilations have taken place this year

Britain recorded 160 alleged cases of 'horse-ripping' between 1983 and 1993.
Daily Telegraph August 28, 2020

What happened to the horse in the poem actually happened to the horse of a friend.

xxiv

'See, they return'… from Ezra Pound's poem, 'The Return':

See, they return, one, and by one,
With fear, as half-awakened…

… 'not quite yet//undone by death': reference to Eliot's *The Waste Land*, where 'A crowd flowed over London Bridge, so many/I had not thought death had undone so many.'

XXV

Police horse bolts as London anti-racism protests turn violent

The Telegraph, 7 June, 2020

Luna: personification of the moon as a goddess worshipped at the new and full moons. English Police Horses are traditionally given names of Gods or Goddesses, or of famous warriors in history.

Epona: a Gaulish goddess who was, among other things, in charge of taking care of horsemen and the cavalry. All over Gallia there were Epona temples where people traditionally offered up freshly cut roses or rose petals to their goddess.

Sefton (1963–1993), born in Co Waterford, Ireland, was a British Army horse who served for 17 years from 1967 to 1984, coming to prominence when he was critically injured in the Hyde Park and Regent's Park IRA bombings which, combined, killed seven other horses and eleven people.

Epilogue:

'Hear them//dictate, from some castle turret'… Rilke felt that the *Duino Elegies* – began in 1912 at Duino Castle where he was the guest of Princess Marie von Thurn und Taxis-Hohenlohe – were somehow dictated to him by the angels. He left the elegies until 1922 and wrote them in a great rush in a 'hurricane of the spirit' at the Chateau de Muzot in Veyras, Switzerland. Rilke's *Duino Elegies* are 'life-saving' poems.

Also by Patricia McCarthy:

Survival (Lovejoy Press, US., 1975)

A Second Skin (Peterloo Poets, 1985)

Rainer Maria Rilke's *Book of Hours*,
    translated by Patricia McCarthy and
    Christine McNeill, (Agenda Editions, 2007)

Rodin's Shadow (Clutag Press/Agenda Editions, 2012)

Horses Between Our Legs (Agenda Editions, 2014)

Letters to Akhmatova (Waterloo Press/Agenda Editions, 2015)

Trodden Before (The High Window Press, 2018)

Rockabye (Worple Press, 2018)

Round the Mulberry Bush (Waterloo Press, 2021)

Hand in Hand (London Magazine Editions 2021)